Holy Spirit

God Bless
Nysley D_____

He's Awesome!

NYSLEY DINNALL

Guardian
B O O K S

Belleville, Ontario, Canada

The Holy Spirit (in a Nutshell) He's Awesome!

Copyright © 2002, Nysley Dinnall

ISBN: 1-55306-392-9

**For more information or
to order additional copies, please contact:**

Nysley Dinnall
179 Ravenscroft Rd.
Ajax, ON L1T 1Z9

Guardian Books is an imprint of *Essence Publishing,* a Christian Book Publisher dedicated to furthering the work of Christ through the written word. For more information, contact:

44 Moira Street West, Belleville, Ontario, Canada K8P 1S3.
Phone: 1-800-238-6376. Fax: (613) 962-3055.
E-mail: info@essencegroup.com
Internet: www.essencegroup.com

Printed in Canada
by
Guardian
B O O K S

Table of Contents

What Changes Does He Bring About in Our Lives?

Acknowledgements

OVER THE YEARS, I HAVE BEEN blessed with some special people in my life. Their contribution to the physical, spiritual, emotional, and social areas in my life is greatly appreciated.

To my children—Brian, Alicia, and Caroline—who gave me the inspiration to fight on through their zest and pride which are consistently demonstrated by a thumbs-up or a favourite rap—"Go Mummy, go Mummy…." To my husband, Lester, who always supports me in whatever I do and whose financial contribution helps make this achievement possible. I love you, Honey.

To people like my grandparents (God rest their souls), especially my grandmother who, in spite of difficult times, insisted I go to school and get an education. To my aunt, Yvonne Reid, who took the place of a mom very early in life and whose hilarious jokes and gestures made me laugh.

Thanks to Marie Lewis whose encouraging words have been a tower of strength and motivation.

Special thanks to Minister McCarthy who contributed to this endeavour by sharing his thoughts, encouragement, and study materials, all of which came in handy in my writing. God bless you.

To my pastor, Reverend Joseph Fisher, the shepherd and founder of the Word of Truth Christian Centre, whose uplifting, inspiring words, preaching, and teaching are tremendously appreciated.

To the people who are responsible for coordinating the *King James Study Bible* and *Bible Readings for the Home*; many thanks for the opportunity to have these books to study and educate ourselves.

Last, but by no means least, to the caring ministers, brothers and sisters in Christ, friends and extended family members (including Phillip Reid who is like a son to me) who have touched my life through their tremendous influence and encouragement, both physically and spiritually. God bless you and thanks from the bottom of my heart. *To God be the glory.*

Why This Book Was Written

Ⓐ T DOES NOT MATTER HOW strong we are or, for that matter, whether or not we are saved, we all need the Holy Spirit in our lives—*all* of us. I realize some have the basic knowledge of the Holy Spirit but not in a *shekinah* way. The Hebrew word *shekinah* means, "dwelling of God."[1] It is the heart-felt presence of God among His people, a presence that is powerful and rich. We can experience God's *shekinah* glory through the Holy Spirit.

There is a difference in the way the Spirit operates in the Old Testament and in the New Testament. The Holy Spirit came upon believers or spoke to them as a presence in the Old Testament, while in the New Testament believers experienced the infilling of the Holy Spirit. The prophets of old foresaw and prophesied the coming of the Messiah who would bring about the outpouring and infilling of the Holy Spirit (Joel 2:28-29; Num. 11:16-17;

Acts 2:4,17-18). Most of us do not experience the deep rooting of the Spirit. The need to fathom His awesomeness is very lacking in the lives of many Christians.

I experienced the moving of the Spirit in a gushing way at a particular time in my life, and I was asked some questions by a few believers, including the pastor of my church at the time. I felt attacked. One of the questions was, "Did God tell you to run around the church?" If these people were in tune with the Holy Spirit or had a clear understanding of the moving of the Holy Spirit, I believe they would not have asked me such questions. Other questions were asked, but if answers had been given, they might not have been believed anyway, because flesh cannot comprehend spiritual things.

The reality is, the Holy Spirit is not a natural person, He is a spirit being, He is a presence. Thus, questions pertaining to our physical, natural selves cannot necessarily be answered where the Spirit is concerned. Sometimes the Spirit uses a person as a vessel to pass on a message to someone else; you don't have to know who the message belongs to, but you are just the vessel carrying it. A person might recognize something that was said by someone through the Spirit and talk with God privately about that situation. Sometimes He can't be explained word for word. He is an invisible person, He is mysterious, He is the Holy Spirit.

The interrogation I mentioned brought me to my knees immediately after it occurred. I fasted and prayed for seven days during the following week, and so I had a great urge to write about the Holy Spirit and the experiences I have with Him in my life. After a great deal of research and studying of the Word, I began to wish I had all this information previously. Nevertheless, trials and testing are good for the soul. They bring us to heights we never imagined we could achieve.

Another fact is, the Spirit relates and operates in different ways to different people, so the need was eminent to include other Christian's views, experiences, and perspectives about the Holy Spirit; thus this book was born. I believe many believers will receive added insights on the move of the Spirit by reading this book, and *to God be the glory*!

——Notes——

[1]Donald C. Stamps, *The Full Life Study Bible, KJV* (Zondervan Publishing House, 1992) p. 1186.

Foreword

MUCH HAS BEEN WRITTEN and said over the years about the Holy Spirit. We have not and cannot exhaust all that could be trumpeted about the Holy Spirit. Indeed, "He is awesome"!

As you read through these pages, you will see that Minister Nysley Dinnall brings to life several aspects of the work of the Holy Spirit, using sound doctrinal truths and personal experiences to underscore the declaration that the third person of the Godhead is "awesome."

After reading this book, you will be assured that because of the regenerative and enabling power of the Holy Spirit, you can now:

✳ obtain eternal life

✳ enter into the presence of God with boldness

❈ render the works of darkness ineffective and power-less

❈ triumph over the many challenges of life

❈ speak into being things that are not, as though they were

And the list continues!

This book shows its readers that a relationship with the Holy Spirit is a vital ingredient in the recipe for maintaining a connection to God.

Minister Nysley Dinnall has now added to the library of great works on the subject of the Holy Spirit. The Apostle Paul would be proud.

~Rev. Joseph G. Fisher

THE INVISIBLE WAR

I face this struggle everyday
with the inner and outer man, I would say.
They never slumber nor do they sleep,
they're constantly in battle, never at peace.

One sees my triumph, strength, and tenacity,
the other sees my failure, weakness, and lack of activity.
I woke up to a beautiful, sunshiny day
with glittering hope as I made time to pray.
I yawned and stretched as one said,
"This is the day the Lord has made."
Sure enough, the other replied,
"And this is the day that bill must be paid."

One tries to do good and kind deeds,
the other combats the good with evil and succeeds.
Throughout the day, the war swiftly
transfers to the mind;
One pursues thoughts of honesty, truth,
loveliness, and purity,
The other counteracts with unfairness, lies,
ugliness, and obscurity.

I can't tell them to leave, nor can I run away.
As long as I'm here, they are here to stay.
Shh… one's talking:
"Walk in the Spirit and you will not fulfill the lust of the flesh."
The other says,
"You can't do that. How are you to walk in the Spirit?"
The other replies,

*"Silly, I meant concentrate, focus, love the things of God,
then you will not be drawn to the things of the world."
The other says,
"I'll give you ten seconds, no, I'll give you a whole minute
and you'll be back in my lure."*

*Suddenly, the point of testing arrives
as a brightly lit bulb goes off in my mind.
The glamour of fashion catches my eyes;
I have a wedding coming soon, what great buys!
"Your closet at home is full," says one,
"with hardly room for anything else.
Don't put yourself in debt and cause more pain for yourself."*

*"Wow! Look at that gorgeous, hunk of a guy!
I would tell him so, if only I wasn't shy."
"Don't forget," says the other, "there's one in your life.
You just need to take a closer look, being his wife."*

*Thank you, positive one,
I'm glad you're there to hold my hand
amidst the trials and tests,
the struggles and pain,
the battles in the home, in the workplace,
in the church, in the street—boy, I need grace!
You never fail to steer me right
as you whisper solid instructions,
though not without a fight.*

*If I would only listen to you, Holy Spirit,
each day I'd be victorious and triumph in God's merit!*

~NYSLEY DINNALL

PART 1

Who Is He?

CHAPTER ONE

His Existence

THE HOLY SPIRIT IS THE THIRD person in the Godhead, also known as the three-in-one or triune God. We find the Holy Ghost and the Holy Spirit mentioned in the Bible. They are described by different Scriptures than the other members of the Godhead because of the differing contexts, but they remain the same entity.

The Holy Spirit existed from the beginning. Genesis 1:2 says, *"...the Spirit of God was hovering over the waters"* (NIV). Notice that God was present there, but so was the Holy Spirit, and each had a part to play in creation. The Spirit (a presence) in this case *moved* upon the waters, while God (the Father) did the talking. The Hebrew word *ruah*, which is spirit, is translated to mean "wind and breath." Again, these are words which describe the Holy Spirit.

Jesus said in John 3:8,

The wind blows wherever it pleases. You hear its sound, but you cannot tell where it comes from or where it is going (NIV).

The Spirit has the same mystery about Him as the wind. He has feelings and emotions. He was upset with the Israelites when they rebelled against Him. He was grieved, He was mad. Is He any different today? Does He illustrate different qualities in the past than in the present? No! He is always the same. It was revealed to David by the Holy Ghost that Jesus Christ is Lord:

For David himself said by the Holy Ghost, The LORD *said to my Lord, Sit thou on my right hand, till I make thine enemies thy footstool* (Mark 12:36).

The Spirit also existed in the lives of the judges of Israel. They were not baptized with Him, but they were supernaturally empowered by Him, and thus did wonders and amazing works in their time.

Let's take a look at Gideon: *"...the Spirit of the* LORD *came upon Gideon"* (Judg. 6:34). He experienced the power of the Holy Spirit who strengthened him and directed him to lead God's people. Gideon was very humble and he was poor. He considered himself to be the least of his family. He saw and experienced the oppression of the Midianites on the children of Israel and was concerned. It was at this time God visited him and told him he was a brave man, and God used him to save Israel.

When I was growing up, I felt like Gideon. I considered myself to be the "black sheep of the family." I was last on the ladder of favouritism, yet I experienced God's abundant provision and love in many ways. He placed people in my life who helped build my character, self-esteem, and love for God. I owe a lot to many of my brothers and sisters in the Lord who still live in Jamaica.

God used base things to confound the wisdom of this world. I can testify to this because He used me in many ways: in singing, teaching, giving, and living an exemplary life in Christ. Over the years, I've been a blessing to many by the grace of God, especially in my singing ministry. People would come to me after a performance with encouragement and appreciation of how blessed they felt when I sang. One thing I'm happy about is that I can take credit for nothing because only God could have used me to be a blessing. He favoured me, and one of the jobs of the Holy Spirit is to direct us in our walk with God and in our endeavours.

Look at Jephthah, another judge of Israel: *"Then the Spirit of the LORD came upon Jephthah, and he passed over Gilead..."* (Judg. 11:29). Jephthah was victorious over the children of Ammon against whom he fought. This came about through the working of the Spirit of the Lord. Thus, another job of the Holy Spirit is to bring victory.

Let's look at Samson, the strongest man who ever lived. It is evident that the Spirit of the Lord was with Samson: *"And the Spirit of the LORD began to move him at times in the camp of Dan between Zorah and Eshtaol"* (Judg. 13:25). Samson allowed the beauty and charm of a woman (Delilah) to cause him to disobey God and lost the purpose for which he was born. Nevertheless, the acknowledgement of his sins caused him to return to God. This is when I believe the Holy Spirit started visiting him again. In the end he won the battle against his enemies. God's will must be accomplished, and at times it takes the moving of the Holy Spirit to set things in order.

Oftentimes, we are determined to choose our own way, but the Spirit will move us when He needs to do so. We can hold out on the Lord all we want. Sometimes we refuse to praise Him or be grateful to Him for His goodness and mercy in our lives, but He's still in control and in His timing. He can move us to do those things He's required of us to do. He has the power to move us! Samson was strong—not necessarily because of the food he ate or tonics he drank, but because the Spirit was a valuable part of his life.

There are countless other prophets and people of God who were empowered by the Spirit. As you search the Scriptures, you will become familiar with them. Obviously, He existed long ago, but He also exists in this present time. The Holy Spirit lives in us. The circumstances of today may be different than they were in Bible times, but He is very much present in our world with the same power as of old. He never, ever loses His power. Hallelujah!

HOW HE EXISTS TODAY

The Spirit lives in our hearts. He is a part of our lives.

Jesus answered, "I tell you the truth, no one can enter the kingdom of God unless he is born of water and the Spirit. Flesh gives birth to flesh, but the Spirit gives birth to spirit....The wind blows wherever it pleases. You hear its sound, but you cannot tell where it comes from or where it is going. So it is with everyone born of the Spirit" (John 3:5-6,8 NIV).

I am certain of the Holy Spirit's residence in my heart because of the transformation He has brought about in my active life. My attitude is different; I'm governed by a positive and godly attitude. Therefore, the reflection of this change causes growth, prosperity, and a life that testifies to others—not necessarily by spoken word, but by my moral actions and good deeds.

Once I was approached by one of my neighbours with a comment I considered the highlight of that day. He said, "I really admire you and your family. Your children are so well-mannered, and I notice you all go to church every Sunday. That is what I would like for my family."

I gave him a few encouraging words and reminded him of how important it is to grow our children up to love the Lord at an early age. I didn't know he was paying such close attention to our lifestyle as a family. Then I thought, if he was noticing us, there were probably others who shared the same observations and kept to themselves. Your lifestyle can be a testimony; live for Jesus every day.

I recall another time my neighbour came over and said, "How is it your grass is so green?" We had moved in only a few months before and did not adequately care for the lawn. Other lawns were looking dry, but somehow, even without proper care, our lawn looked green and healthy. I thought to myself, *God does takes care of His people, even their grass!* (I hear a chuckle.)

Since that time, I have noticed a change in the lives of that family. Almost every Sunday, they go to church—talk about lives influencing other lives! We can come to the conclusion that the Spirit is mysterious. The man born of the Spirit has a mystery tag on him. That's why the man who is not governed by the Spirit cannot understand the moving of the Spirit and so asks questions that are of the flesh. Such questions would not surface if they were in harmony with the Spirit. It's not always wise to doubtfully question the moving of the Spirit; He is a mystery!

I can boldly say, without a shadow of doubt, the Holy Spirit plays a vital role in my life. He comforts me when I'm feeling discouraged and lonely. And when I'm faced with circumstances that cause pain, fear, or frustration, He visits me and immediately there's a presence that brings peace, hope, and boldness.

CHAPTER TWO

His Character

T HE HOLY SPIRIT IS A PERSON. He produces many characteristics which we call *"the fruit of the Spirit"* (Gal. 5:22). The first fruit—love—is, no doubt, one of the most important fruits of the Spirit. When love is developed in a child of God through the Spirit, there is no one on the face of this earth that is impossible to love genuinely. Love overrides fault and failure. When love looks, through the eyes of a Spirit-filled person, at a poor man, it sees riches; when it looks at the homeless, it sees a valuable soul who needs to be caressed; when it looks at the less fortunate, it feels pity and a hunger to give comfort; when it looks at the starving, it's filled with compassion and a need to help. Love doesn't scorn the indifferent, but reaches out to them with the very best service it can offer.

"[Love] *is not rude…*" (1 Cor. 13:5 NIV). Love does not behave in an indecent manner. When you have love, you maintain a good character and become an example for all to emulate. When we have love in our hearts, we choose to speak no ill of our brothers and sisters or anyone for that matter. We behave right. Therefore, I'll ask this question: why is it that (probably) 99 percent of Christian believers don't exemplify this fruit called love? Maybe we are looking at love one-sidedly (at the side that doesn't count for very much). We love those who look like us. We are friendly to those who are easy to love, those who can relate to us. What if one day a person with a severe handicap or a disease or some other serious ailment came in contact with us? How would we react? Would we stay as far away from that person as we could, or would we see them in love through the eyes of the Spirit? Stop and think about this for a minute. Love is more than what we feel for our families and friends. Love reaches out to the worst of the worst. As the Bible says, this special gift of the Spirit *"covers over a multitude of sins"* (1 Pet. 4:8 NIV).

The Spirit is not always a serious, stern person or presence. And He is certainly not boring. In fact, the Holy Spirit shows He has a whole spectrum of actions and emotions in His character. For example, sometimes He makes us laugh, cry, run, dance, or shout. Other times He comes with other languages. Sometimes He overwhelms us from within. And then there are moments He comes in a still, small voice.

It is not easy to laugh or even smile when you are experiencing difficulties or problems of some sort. How can you face eviction from your home and still keep a smile? What keeps a smile on your face when you don't know where the next meal is coming from? How is it that when there is no money in the bank, you are able to smile at someone passing you on the street? Job 5:22 says, *"At destruction and famine thou shalt laugh: neither shalt thou be afraid of the beasts of the earth."* The flesh determines you are not supposed to be pleasant when things are going wrong in your life. "I'm all you've got," the flesh might say. "If I fail you, there's no one else." The Spirit says, "You are not your own. You belong to Jesus and are never alone."

One day, I'll make an exciting entrance into the Kingdom of God. After all is accomplished on this vast earth, there is a beautiful hope to enjoy. After saying hello and being ignored, after those I greet pretend they don't hear or see me, after I feel my self-esteem shattered because I am not good enough to associate with, after certain stares say, "Stay away, I don't want you near me," after I'm sneakily kept from activities because I do not fit the status quo, after I'm mocked, laughed at, scorned, and whispered about—there is *hope*. These things do not happen because I am unhealthy; my yearly doctor's exam gives me a clean bill of health. They happen because I'm not perfect. In fact, not one of us is perfect. We all have some imperfections, inside or outside, yet we treat each other as if one is better than the other. The culprit is the enemy of our souls—the devil. We allow him to use us too often. But one day, one glorious day after all this, I shall make my entrance into the Kingdom of God with all its splendour, and I shall be welcomed with open arms. This is my hope.

The Spirit of the Lord turns the negative into positive every time. Isaiah 61:3 states,

> *To appoint unto them that mourn in Zion, to give unto them beauty for ashes, the oil of joy for mourning, the garment of praise for the spirit of heaviness; that they might be called trees of righteousness, the planting of the Lord that he might be glorified.*

Indeed, the Spirit of the Lord does make a difference in our lives. He causes us to cry sometimes, but what kind of tears do we cry through the Spirit? Most likely, they are not sad tears, but joyous tears, forgiving tears, repentant tears, tears of receiving salvation and gratitude for where you are in Christ compared to where you could have been.

"*When he maketh inquisition for blood, he remembereth them: he forgets not the cry of the humble*" (Ps. 9:12). When you are in the presence of the Holy Spirit, you sometimes feel like running. This is most common in many Pentecostal churches. The excitement and thrill of the songs and music triggers a watering of the Holy Spirit in our hearts, which causes us to run, jump, raise our hands, and praise the Lord for the many things He's done for us and the freedom we have in our lives through Him. There is a lightness about running in the Spirit; it's as if you are being hushed by the wind. Look at 1 Corinthians 9:26: "*I therefore so run, not as uncertainly; so fight I, not as one that beateth the air.*" Outside the realm of the Spirit, you can feel the weight of your body as you run. It is not as easy as running in the Spirit. Then there is an unexplained lightness in your physical body, especially when you are manifesting in the Spirit. Try the same move in the natural and you will realize it's far more difficult to do. "Why?" you may ask. I'm not sure I can give you the perfect answer. It is possible that as you allow Him to control your heart and mind, He diminishes fear and any other hindrances in that moment.

Here's an example: I have pain in my left knee whenever I sit for long periods or engage in any kind of activity that would irritate it. Interestingly, when I am rejoicing in the Spirit, I can jump, run, skip—you name it, and I don't feel any pain. It's like an out-of-body experience when I'm focused on the Spirit.

When a person dances in the Spirit, it's a dance that is sweet. There is a feeling of boldness, godly pride, and joy, and it feels as if you are transformed to a different realm. Believers manifesting in the Spirit often take risky jumps or runs (so it seems when looking on) and they don't hurt anyone or themselves. This is truly amazing! The Spirit moves in mysterious ways, His wonders to perform.

I love to sing in the Spirit; it's an awesome feeling with which nothing can compare. As I focus on the words of the song, keeping my mind on heaven and staying under the anointing of the Spirit, I feel like I'm in heavenly places. Oh... what joy! I pray everyone could experience this great feeling.

Shouting in the Spirit is like a quickening:

For Christ also hath once suffered for sins, the just for the unjust, that he might bring us to God, being put to death in the flesh, but quickened by the Spirit (1 Pet. 3:18).

You experience what seems like electricity—a sudden shock—deep down in your heart, and you burst out with, "Hallelujah!" Or you might shout, "Jesus! Glory! Yes, Lord! Praise God! My Lord!" etc. When this quickening occurs, you feel as if you have all the power from on high. This high does not cause sickness or hangovers; it brings peace, joy, and an eagerness to face the next day. The most bashful or timid person experiencing this awesome feeling might run, skip, march (you name it) around the place of worship because liberty accompanies this experience. Praise God! Hallelujah! I feel like skipping right now!

Many people have a problem with saints who shout and/or move in the Spirit, but God can choose to use a person in whatever capacity He pleases in order to perform or carry out His will. Reason with me: if someone is electrified with even the least amount of electrical power, or if a hot coal fell in his shoes, could that person stand still? No, of course not. He's going to jump up, jiggle, scream, or roll. Whatever the case, he's going to react to such an incident.

Experiencing the Holy Spirit is similar. He's like a volcano bubbling up inside because the Spirit works on the heart and soul. Therefore, when you become overwhelmed with this power, you've got to give way to Him. A minority of folks do go to some extremes in the manifestation of the Spirit. He is wise, but He's not a brawler. He does not go outside the Word of God. Remember, everything must be done in decency and with order. *For God hath not given us the spirit of fear; but of power, and of love, and of a sound mind* (2 Tim. 1:7).

Nevertheless, David was once so overwhelmed in his spirit that he took off his clothes and danced before the Ark of the Lord. In today's world, he would be looked on as an insane person, but God uses whom he pleases, and in whatever way He pleases, to show His glory. We do not have to question Him. We might not always understand Him, but He's God, and He alone is in control.

When Jesus took Peter, James, and John to the Mount of Transfiguration, it's safe to say the presence of God was there because the Bible says Jesus' garments became shining and white as snow. This presence was so extraordinary, it caused Peter to utter things he shouldn't have said. The fact is, he became confused (Mark 9:2-8) and overwhelmed by what he saw.

Speaking in tongues is a controversy to many, and some reasons for skepticism may be legitimate. Nevertheless, the Bible proves that speaking in tongues plays a very important part in the life of a Spirit-filled believer because it is one of the initial evidences of the infilling of the Holy Spirit. In other words, it is one of the manifestations that proves you have the Spirit.

There is a mystery in tongues. Personally, I find I usually speak in tongues when I am empowered by the Spirit and mere words are insufficient for what I really want to express to God. Understand this: speaking in tongues is not, and should not be a selfish, fleshly, shallow form of worship. It is a soul experience. This is why the man who is in the flesh or out of touch with the Spirit cannot understand this. Acts 2:1-4 tells us that the Holy Spirit came to the disciples as a strong wind, and tongues of fire touched each disciple assembled there. They then began to talk in other languages (now this is very important), *"as the Spirit enabled them"* (NIV). They were speaking under the influence and direction of the Holy Spirit. Verse 11 says, *"we do hear them speak in our tongues the wonderful works of God."* In Acts 19:6, we find the Holy Spirit, with His miraculous power, working through a man of God:

> *When Paul placed his hands on them, the Holy Spirit came on them, and they spoke in tongues and prophesied* (NIV).

There are principles that govern speaking in tongues. One is found in 1 Corinthians 12:8,10:

> *To one there is given through the Spirit... speaking in different kinds of tongues, and to still another the interpretation of tongues* (NIV).

You see, every gift has its rightful place in the Church. The Bible mentions in 1 Corinthians 12:28 that there are *"diversities of tongues"*; they all do not sound the same, neither are they manifested in the same manner. All are geared according to the direction of the Spirit. Here's another rule, found in 1 Corinthians 14:27: *"If anyone speaks in a tongue, two—or at the most three—should speak, one at a time..."* (NIV). There must be order and not confusion in the manifestation of the Holy Spirit.

Here's another principle: if there is no interpreter, the person should speak quietly to God. There is the possibility that the one who speaks in tongues can also interpret.

The Bible says that God gives us gifts, and *"gives them to each one, just as he determines"* (1 Cor. 12:11 NIV).

Let's look at two further principles for the public use of spiritual gifts:

> *And if a revelation comes to someone who is sitting down, the first speaker should stop* (1 Cor. 14:30 NIV).

> *The spirits of prophets are subject to the control of prophets* (1 Cor. 14:32 NIV).

To close this chapter, verse 40 says, *"But everything should be done in a fitting and orderly way"* (NIV). I couldn't phrase it any better.

CHAPTER THREE

His Individuality and Identity

His Individuality

THE HOLY SPIRIT DEALS WITH EACH OF US in His own unique way. He is individualized in our lives, meaning we will not all sing the same way or with the same results, nor will we preach, teach, move, or speak identically. We are all individuals with different abilities, personalities, and emotions. Therefore, the Spirit deals or communicates with us on our own levels. The Scripture shows us how the Spirit deals with individuals even in the strangest and most unusual ways. Let's go on a journey and see this magnificent picture unfold.

Personal Experience in the Spirit

I'll fill you in on one of my life's stories. I recall this event as clear as crystal because it happened to me at a significant time in my life. I was about twenty-four years old and single when a man came into my life. In my eyes, he was the ideal man, one I believe any young woman would have wanted to marry. He was handsome, intelligent, witty, and a good conversationalist. I was in love!

We became close friends and decided to get engaged, but it was not to be. All communication broke off, and we did not follow through with the engagement. The bottom line was I was devastated and turned to the one person who could help me—God. This was what I prayed to Him: "Dear Lord, I feel like I can't go on because I'm hurting and my heart is bleeding here alone. I wonder, Lord, what I did to deserve this, so I'm calling on you to help me understand." I cried, but I didn't feel like it was helping. I asked "why," but the answer never came. Then, with all the power I had in me, I yelled at the top of my lungs as if there was no more tomorrow, "Jesus, I'm calling you. Don't leave me, I'm falling. Come quickly and help me; hold me, dear Lord." With tears falling down and my head aching from built-up pressure, I got up feeling refreshed and strengthened.

From that day on, I emphasized this in my prayers: "Lord, you choose my mate. Whoever you give, I will accept." Guess what? He did choose my mate. My husband Lester is a wonderful man. He knew of my many faults and weaknesses, high and low points in my life, yet these did not prevent him from loving me; this is undoubtedly one of the stimuli that kep me persistent, especially in our marriage. Many times, when I felt like giving up on our marriage because of depression and frustration from my own insecurities, Lester would say,

"I'm not letting you go. I love you, just trust in God." The Lord knew who I needed, and He gave him to me.

God does hear and answer prayer, so to all single ladies and men, let God be your first priority and the Holy Spirit your guide, and I promise you will marry the one who truly belongs to you.

Isaiah 61:3 talks about *the oil of joy for mourning, the garment of praise for the spirit of heaviness.* This is a wonderful scripture with some instructions on how to worship in the Spirit. Praying in the power of the Holy Spirit is an amazing time in the presence of God. The most successful prayer one will ever have through the Spirit is when, previous to praying, he or she spends some time in the Word of God. When you fill your heart with the Word, you'll be able to pray using the Word. The Spirit cannot operate on what is not there; He needs the Word—they go together. When I pray focusing on heaven and the sacrifice Christ made for me on the cross of Calvary and thinking about His goodness, I suddenly find myself in another presence. It is when you could say you feel "sweet in Jesus." There's no feeling like it!

Praising God in the Spirit is a form of worship I enjoy. It can be emotional sometimes. It's like a force coming up from the inside that I don't want to quench. I want to give it all with all my heart. Here's a more vivid picture: you're at a ball game and your team is down by 5. It's a 5-0 score. Then your team comes up to bat, and before the inning is ended, you get a grand slam. Would you stop to check who is around before you cheer from the depths of your lungs? I don't think so. The excitement of the moment, the electricity of the crowd, and the desire to win would cause you to shout, "Woo hoo, alright, go Blue Jays!" (that's my favourite baseball team). Now do you get the picture?

As I praise God for His goodness and blessings in my life and in the life of my family; when I think how much I've failed Him and how inadequate I am before Him and how He still cares and shows His mercy everyday, then oh... I feel compelled to burst out with, "Hallelujah! Glory!" and tears of joy, thanks, and gratitude. These tears are filled with questions. "Why do you love me so much when I'm so undeserving? What have I done to gain your mercies? What can I do to make up for what you did for me on Calvary?" My attitude toward everyone becomes filled with humility, compassion, respect, love, and I feel like a millionaire!

HIS IDENTITY

Perhaps the most important thing to know about the Holy Spirit is that He is the third person in the Godhead or the Trinity which consists of the Father, Son, and Holy Spirit (Matt. 28:19). His Hebrew name, as I've said before, is *ruah*, meaning wind or breath. Therefore, His identity in the Old Testament books refers to these conditions:

Then said he unto me, Prophesy unto the wind, prophesy, son of man, and say to the wind, Thus saith the Lord GOD; Come from the four winds, O breath, and breathe upon these slain, that they may live. So I prophesied... and they lived, and stood up upon their feet, an exceeding great army (Ezek. 37:9-10).

He is also identified as a living being. He brings life. He is a leader. Without His leading, we would be faced with chaos and problems constantly. He has the greatest power a leader could possess. Gideon experienced His leadership: *"But the Spirit of the LORD came upon Gideon and he blew a trumpet"* (Judg. 6:34). David also had the experience: *"...and the Spirit of the LORD came upon David from that day forward"* (1 Sam. 16:13). No wonder David was able to do exploits for God in his lifetime—the defeat of Goliath, the escape from Saul who wanted to take his life, the many victories he had in the battles he fought for Israel, and much more. The Spirit of the Lord directed his every move. The Holy Spirit is identified in our service to God. Joseph served Pharaoh's political empire very well because he had the Spirit with him. *"And Pharaoh said unto his servants, Can we find such a one as this, a man in whom the Spirit of God is?"* (Gen. 41:38).

Here's a blast to you unbelievers: when the Lord wants to use His people in a great way, He allows the Holy Spirit to come upon them. At Jesus' baptism, the Spirit was identified as a dove that came and sat on Jesus' head, giving Him the maximum endorsement of power, right, and authority to accomplish the Father's will in His ministry. The Spirit loves and enjoys fellowship which is why we cannot leave Him out of our worship and service to God, nor can we leave Him out of our daily lives. He is the One behind the scenes whom we cannot see, who whispers the right things to counteract the wrong. He is our Comforter. If ever you need someone to cheer you up, call on the Holy Spirit. You can count on Him. In anxiety, call Him; in depression, call Him; during trouble in the home, church, workplace, etc., call Him. If you feel lonely and need an arm around you, *call Him.* He'll always be there, and He'll always be on time.

The Holy Spirit is like a sweet aroma in my life. In Matthew 3:16, He is described as a dove. He indwells our hearts and brings us blessings. He causes us to have a heart of gratitude and praise to God.

In John 14:16 and 26, Jesus made a promise to His disciples. He told them,

> *I will pray the Father, and he shall give you another Comforter, that he may abide with you for ever.... But the Comforter, which is the Holy Ghost, whom the Father will send in my name, he shall teach you all things, and bring all things to your remembrance, whatsoever I have said unto you.*

Certainly, He is our Comforter. The Holy Spirit has always been my Comforter. I recall a very sad period in my life in 1992, when I was pregnant with my third child. I had planned to name him Andrew because I was told by the doctor that it was a boy. However, due to a few complications, including a minor accident three months into the pregnancy, I lost the baby. He was stillborn at five months. Prior to losing my baby, I remember lying on my back very late at night in the hospital (I was there so the doctors could monitor the baby) with excruciating pain all through my body. One distraction from the pain and the uncertainty of the result of this pregnancy was a cassette, given to me by a wonderful sister in the Lord, Beverly Johnson. Some of the songs were about the Holy Spirit. As I listened to these songs, my heart was opened to the words, and I felt a wonderful presence as if I was enclosed within the arms of someone. I felt comforted and at peace. Many times in that hospital room, in the stillness of the night, that was how I drifted off to sleep. I found comfort in His arms.

DAVID DANCED IN THE STREETS

David's dancing had to do with the Ark of the Lord. The Ark represented the presence of God. It was feared by David because of the tremendous power it carried with it. A man named Uzzah, who was close by the Ark as it passed by, tried to hold it to keep it from falling, and he died because he was ignorant of the word of God concerning the Ark. Nevertheless, the Ark was a blessing. David found this out as he took note that those who were carrying the Ark were not endangered. Then he stopped and offered sacrifices to God, and in the excitement of the moment and worship, he danced before the Lord with all his might.

Now, some people don't like to see you glorify God, especially when you give of yourself freely and ask the Spirit to have His way in your life. When He starts using us in His way, many find it a problem. People who don't understand might think you are nuts. It was Peter who once told some people that he and his disciples were not drunk but filled with the Spirit (Acts 2:15-18). In David's case, it was Michal, Saul's daughter, that despised him in her heart as he danced. But it didn't stop there. She decided to approach David and question him on the matter. David gave her the perfect answer:

David said unto Michal, It was before the LORD, which chose me before thy father, and before all his house, to appoint me ruler over the people of the LORD, over Israel: therefore will I play before the LORD. And I will be more vile than thus, and will be base in my own sight: and of the maidservants which thou has spoken of, of them shall I be had in honour (2 Sam. 6:21-22).

David knew from where God had taken him. He had been a shepherd boy promoted to king of Israel. He knew why he was praising God.

When someone worships God in sincerity and truth (according to the manifestation), it might not be tasteful to some, but God gets the glory. And if anyone despises, criticizes, or acts displeased with that person's worship to God, there are ramifications which, in one way or another, will be carried out. Michal paid dearly for her criticism towards David. The Bible says in verse 23 she had no children to the day of her death. We have to be careful when it comes to God and His glory. If God can use a donkey to talk as a man (Num. 22), why can't He use a man (even if he acts as a madman) to glorify Him? God can do whatever He pleases to glorify His name. Never underestimate God or the Holy Spirit because they are one.

PETER'S SHADOW

Many of us would be skeptical if we heard of a preacher who came into our town and his shadow healed the sick. We would laugh at the idea. Even if some of us were living in Peter's time, it would be difficult to believe such miraculous power. Well, it did happen! the Bible states, in Acts 5:15,

> *...they brought forth the sick into the streets, and laid them on beds and couches, that at the least the shadow of Peter passing by might over shadow some of them.*

One of the keys to salvation is *belief*. When we believe, we exercise the Spirit in our hearts which also proves His identity in our lives. Do not doubt—believe! Believe especially when things seem impossible and difficult, for *"with God all things are possible"* (Matt. 19:26).

These Scriptures should jog your memory and help you believe: *"Be not afraid, only believe"* (Mark 5:36); *"Believe on the Lord Jesus Christ, and thou shalt be saved"* (Acts 16:31); *"Have ye received the Holy Ghost since ye believed?"* (Acts 19:2); *"I believe that thou art the Christ, the Son of God..."* (John 11:27); *"...for I know whom I have believed, and am persuaded that he is able to keep that which I have committed unto him against that day"* (2 Tim. 1:12); *"...for he that cometh to God must believe that he is, and that he is a rewarder of them that diligently seek him..."* (Heb. 11:6); *"If ye will not believe, surely ye shall not be established"* (Isa. 7:9); *"...Lord I believe: help thou mine unbelief"* (Mark 9:24).

THE BAPTISM OF JESUS

The Holy Spirit was identified as a "dove" at the baptism of Jesus. He had to be there in support of the Son of God:

And Jesus, when he was baptized, went up straitway out of the water: and, lo, the heavens were opened unto him, and he saw the Spirit of God descending like a dove, and lighting upon him: And lo a voice from heaven, saying, This is my beloved Son, in whom I am well pleased (Matt. 3:16-17).

STEPHEN'S DEATH

Stephen was not alone when he died; the Spirit was with him. He was a God-fearing man who was not afraid to preach Jesus to the people in Jerusalem. He performed miracles and wonders among the people to whom he preached. He talked about the history of Israel, including the exodus from Egypt, but his statement in the following verses may have been the dagger to their hardened hearts which caused them to stone him. Ironically, the Spirit was steering him; notice how quickly you can cause an uproar or a stir when you speak the truth under the anointing of the Holy Spirit.

Here's what Stephen said in Acts 7:51-53:

You stiff-necked people, with uncircumcised hearts and ears! You are just like your fathers:. You always resist the Holy Spirit! Was there ever a prophet your fathers did not persecute? They even killed those who preached the coming of the Righteous One. And now you have betrayed and murdered him— you who have received the law that was put into effect through angels but have not obeyed it (NIV).

Wow! They must have been fuming with anger.

In verse 56, a glorious picture was revealed to Stephen. The heavens were opened and he saw Jesus, not sitting at the right hand of God, which would have been the normal setting, but standing to welcome him home. You see, this was an extraordinary occasion, so Jesus stood up for Stephen. Isn't that wonderful? A man who remained faithful to God, even in death, reaped the legacy of being welcomed into the Kingdom of God by no other than the King of Kings and the Lord of Lords.

HE'S A COMFORTER

This is the testimony of Marie Lewis, a beautiful sister in the Lord. She said, "I just want to relate a testimony of how the Holy Ghost, the Comforter, does comfort in the time of great discouragement and anxiety.

"I had been working very long shifts at work and felt drained and exhausted. The weekend came, and it was church as usual. As we were on our way to church, I kept praying in my heart, 'Lord, I am so tired, I just want to be home with you. What are you waiting for, Lord?' I really meant what I was praying; I just felt I'd had it. The service was good, but I was still discouraged and anxious. We went home, had our supper, and I went to rest for a few minutes. It was then the Comforter came and comforted me. The Spirit of the Lord said, 'Get up, take your Bible, and read 2 Corinthians 12:9.' As I took the Bible and read the verse, I had immediate strength. I cannot explain how it happened, but it was wonderful!"

HE'S A PROVIDER

Marie continues her testimony on the Holy Spirit by describing Him as her provider. *"They shall not be ashamed in the evil time: and in the days of famine they shall be satisfied"* (Ps. 37:19).

"I remember I had just gotten married and had my first child," she continues. "My husband was working alone while I stayed home to take care of our son. Life was very hard with one income, but the Lord always provided for us.

"At this particular time we really had no money, not even a penny. It was a Saturday morning and my husband and I got up and went into the living room of our one bedroom apartment and began to pray. After we had finished praying, within the space of half an hour, there was a knock on the door. My husband opened the door and it was a friend who handed him an envelope and left. We celebrated like two excited children, even though we had no clue of what was inside the envelope. We then opened it to find a hundred-dollar bill. Hallelujah! God is good! To make a long story short, we later phoned our friend to inquire why he had brought us this money. He said that while he was in devotion that morning, God spoke to him and told him, 'Take this money over to the Lewis family,' and he obeyed. We were in great need of that money. Indeed, He is a provider."

This motivates me to tell a story of my own of how the Holy Spirit has been my provider. I grew up without a mother or a father's love and care. They did not provide the basic essentials a child needs to function effectively in life. I did not have the luxury of lying in my mother's lap, or of crying on my father's shoulders. I miss that, even now as a grown woman. My mother and father were not at my graduation when I was seventeen years old. I regret not having had them around and truly believe many difficulties and hardships I faced in life could have been prevented. I hold no grudge; I have forgiven them. However, every now and then, I feel the pain and disappointment of them not being a part of my childhood.

Life was a challenge for me growing up. Even from a tender age, I worked very hard lest I be deprived of things I needed. I was reminded I had neither mother nor father, so often I ended up doing chores other family members should have done. Those who know about life in the West Indies can identify with responsibilities such as carrying water on your head from the river for long distances, carrying wood to make fire (we did not own an electric stove), or washing heavy-duty spreads and clothes in aluminum tubs.

I often yearned for love and comfort and for my basic nurturing needs to be fulfilled. And thank God, things changed when I reached the age of thirteen, because that's when I gave my heart to the Lord. It was a beautiful warm Sunday night, and the church was packed to its capacity when the late Pastor Stewart preached a dynamic message and gave an altar call. On previous occasions, I would glance around for a companion to go with me to the altar, but this night it was different. The Word of God must have pierced my heart deeply, because I slowly got up out of my seat, not looking around as before, held my head high and straight, almost as if a gentle force was leading me, and made my way down the isle to the altar. I gave my heart to the Lord. And since that day, I have had no appetite for turning back.

Life became much easier because, whenever I needed comfort or provision in any regard, God was there for me. I cried many times on His shoulders, laid often in His lap, asked countless times for things, and He gave them to me. I remember once I needed a pair of shoes, so I prayed to God, asking Him to provide them for me. Soon after, my Aunt Juanita, who was residing in England, sent a barrel to me containing a pair of shoes and a dress. *God provided!* When I needed to go on trips and had no money, *God provided.* When I needed a job, *God provided.* Everything I needed, He provided and remained faithful.

PART 2

How Does He Operate?

CHAPTER FOUR

He Moves with
Power

POWER OVER SIN

THE SPIRIT GIVES US POWER TO overcome sin. *"This I say then, Walk in the Spirit, and ye shall not fulfill the lust of the flesh"* (Gal. 5:16). The reason so many of us can go to church and sit complacent and comfortable in our seats after committing acts of sin is because of the lack of the Holy Spirit in our hearts and lives.

Some of us go to parties the night before church, drink liquor, smoke, wine and dine, commit sexual immoralities, lie, steal, or covet our neighbours' spouse or possessions. Then we come into church, wipe off our mouths, and put our tails under us (so to speak) like cute little puppies, acting as if nothing happened.

Where are the Spirit-filled, power-packed, Holy Ghost believers who, when the Spirit moves upon them, cause us to shake in our seats or run to the altar or hang our heads in shame with repentant hearts? These days, we are more concerned about people feeling badly than about straightening out their souls for heaven. The Bible says,

> *Now no chastening for the present seemeth to be joyous, but grevious: nevertheless afterward it yieldeth the peaceable fruit of righteousness unto them which are exercised thereby* (Heb. 12:11).

Here's a fact: the flesh and the Spirit perform two different manifestations. The flesh tears down and utters foolishness, but the Spirit convicts, corrects, and build us up.

Do you remember Ananias and Sapphira? Peter discerned, through the Holy Spirit, that their actions were not honest to the promise they had made to the church, and that lie cost them their lives (Acts 5). We have the power to live above sin if we nurture the Spirit in our hearts. God's Word allows the Spirit to grow in our hearts, thus occupying the room He should rightly have in us. *"Thy word have I hid in mine heart, that I might not sin against thee"* (Ps. 119:11).

POWER TO LOVE

I've heard it said that it's not easy to love certain people. In many ways that's true, but it is wonderful to know that, no matter who we are or what we look like, we have the perfect lover. His name is Jesus. We may not be able to love some people; as a matter of fact, some of us can only love our friends or those who like us or smell like us or dress like us. But this perfect lover loves the lowest of the low, the ugliest of the ugly, the dirtiest of the dirty, the vilest of the vile. He's got the power to love (John 3:16). We will never be as perfect in our love, but we can achieve this power: "...*love covers over all wrongs*" (Prov. 10:12 NIV); "*But the fruit of the spirit is love...*" (Gal. 5:22); "*For if ye love them which love you, what reward have ye?*" (Matt. 5:46).

If we pray earnestly for His love to dwell in our hearts, if we invite the Lord into our hearts and feast on His Word, we will have enough love to share so we can love one another genuinely.

POWER TO WITNESS

One of the most powerful commands Jesus gave believers is recorded in Matthew 28:19-20:

> *Go ye therefore, and teach all nations, baptizing them in the name of the Father, and of the Son, and of the Holy Ghost: Teaching them to observe all things whatsoever I have commanded you: and, lo, I am with you always, even unto the end of the world....*

For a great number of believers, witnessing can be a nerve-wracking experience. We become fearful of people rejecting us, slamming doors in our faces, ignoring us, fearful of people challenging us with their own teachings and philosophies which might not be necessarily biblical. But why are we so fearful when we have such secure backing from Christ? He tells us (1.) *Go!* (2.) *Teach!* (3.) *I am with you!* (Matt. 28:19-20). No bodyguard, no matter how strong, can protect us as Jesus can.

Therefore, I ask the question again: why are we so fearful? We need to study His Word and know it like the back of our hands. We need to stand firm on His Word and let no one move us. Be firm as the rock of Gibraltar (my grandmother often used that phrase when she was alive). We need to know our Lord Jesus better.

Get to know Him just as you would your spouse, children, or parents. Finally, be confident in who you are in Christ Jesus. When you focus on the God you serve—the King of Kings, Lord of Lords, the God of the whole universe—you feel like a giant, and there's nothing you can't do when you put your trust in Him. In fact, you *"can do all things through Christ which strengtheneth"* you (Phil 4:13).

The Holy Spirit gives us compassionate hearts for those living in sin. If we maintain this compassion, we will feel compelled to witness to them using either the Word of God, or a song, testimony, or kind deed. Sometimes our very lives can be a witness. After the eunuch heard the word of God in Acts 8:29-35, he was able to say, in verse 36: *"See, here is water; what doth hinder me to be baptized?"*

POWER TO SERVE

The new convert who accepts the Lord in his heart and gets baptized will feel a great desire to work for God. It does not matter how insignificant the task is, the willingness to be a servant of God overrides that.

Our service is very important in the Kingdom of God. We all as individuals have capabilities to serve. To demonstrate my meaning, let me share with you an example from my own life.

I had not been on the singing team in church for a while. One evening, the song leader of the team was unable to come to church, so the pastor asked me to lead for the night. I nervously obeyed. After church, sister Verna Terrolonge said to me, "The singing team is like a puzzle. You were missing in the puzzle, and so it was not complete. Now that you are back, your piece of puzzle is right where it belongs."

This statement can be applied to our own spiritual walk with God. We *all* have our place in the vast puzzle of God's Kingdom. No one can fill your space, for you are a unique individual. Just look around in our churches at those who faithfully and genuinely serve the cause of Christ. Or look at the extraordinary men and women in the Bible who served, risking and giving up their very lives for the cause of Christ. Many of these people were constantly led by the power of the Holy Spirit, and they followed in obedience, regardless of the consequences.

POWER TO HEAL

A crippled man sat at the gate Beautiful. Perhaps he wished a thousand times to walk as others were able to. He may have gone to all the healing meetings he heard of in town, by whatever means he could get there—but all in vain. However, one day, hope came through the compassion of two sanctified Christian brothers. Peter walked up to him in the power of the Holy Ghost and said, *"Silver and gold have I none; but such as I have give I thee: In the name of Jesus Christ of Nazareth rise up and walk"* (Acts

3:6). The crippled man got his miracle and was healed at that very moment.

This is just one example of the power of healing. But the Bible shows us many more examples of people healed through the power of the Holy Spirit.

Nowadays, many of us underestimate the power of healing. We seem to believe it doesn't happen in today's society, only in times past. This couldn't be further from the truth.

"Verily, verily, I say unto you, He that believeth on me, the works that I do shall he do also; and greater works than these shall he do; because I go unto my Father (John 14:12).

The Spirit is no different now than He was in the apostles' days. He remains the same. *We* change, *we* lack, *we* fall short, *we* refuse to exercise our faith or be led by the Holy Spirit. If we lack these things, how can the power of the Holy Spirit dwell with us? We need Him and His power in our lives to accomplish great things for God.

But the Comforter, which is the Holy Ghost, whom the Father will send in my name, he shall teach you all things, and bring all things to your remembrance, whatsoever I have said unto you (John 14:26).

POWER TO SUCCEED

If I had told some people I was writing a book, they probably would look at me with disbelief. It is not that

I'm not capable, but man's judgment is different from God's judgment. Thank God for that! The fact is, they don't know what I am made of on the inside, but God knows. I knew I already had the power within; I simply needed to listen, be obedient, and move forward with determination and hard work with my goal always in plain view. Finally, through the guidance of the Holy Spirit, I had the power to succeed.

God wants us to succeed and to stop making excuses for being unsuccessful. Philippians 1:6 reads,

Being confident of this very thing, that he which hath began a good work in you will perform it until the day of Jesus Christ.

Can you write songs? Do it. Can you sew? Sew for success. Are you a talker? Make it worth your while. Do you have lots of compassion? Then work with the unfortunate because therein might lie your success.

Whatsoever thy hand findeth to do, do it with thy might; for there is no work, nor device, nor knowledge, nor wisdom, in the grave, whither thou goest (Eccl. 9:10).

CHAPTER FIVE

He Speaks to Individuals

Sometimes the Holy Spirit has a message to deliver to either an individual or a group. The messenger may not have a clue who it is for or what the situation is about. He is only the one the Spirit chose to use for that particular delivery. The postman is a basic example of this explanation. His job is to deliver letters. He doesn't know the person who the letter is going to or the content of the letter; that is not his prerogative. His only concern is to get that letter in the right mailbox. So it is at times with the Holy Spirit.

Don't get me wrong; I know there are times He reveals what He wants to say to an individual. Other times He doesn't, but the message will be understood or known by the recipient—guaranteed! The Holy Spirit can move in a calm way like a soothing breeze or wind, or speak to us in a *"still small voice"* (1 Kings 19:12). He also can take on the force of a stronger wind like a hurricane and pull up strongholds or shatter the devil's kingdom. He is not a weakling; He is *power!*

The Spirit does not always comes with loud shouting or great noise. He is wise in His operations. Some situations and circumstances vary, and so the Spirit matches each accordingly. For instance, if you are experiencing a sad or grieving time in your life, He's not going to come banging you over your head, saying, "Come on, pick yourself up and be on your way." He's not cruel; He knows you arc hurting. His instinct is to speak to you in a still small voice with soothing and encouraging words. He might bring to your heart words like these: *"The Lord lift up his countenance upon thee and give thee peace"* (Num. 6:26); *"Peace be both to thee, and peace be to thine house, and peace be unto all that thou hast"* (1 Sam. 25:6); *"For he is our peace..."* (Eph. 2:14); *"Casting all your care upon him; for he careth for you"* (1 Pet. 5:7); *"I can do all things through Christ which strengtheneth me"* (Phil. 4:13); *"Trust in the LORD with all thine heart; and lean not unto thine own understanding"* (Prov. 3:5); *"Let not your heart be troubled: ye believe in God, believe also in me"* (John 14:1).

A biblical example of a "still small voice" is the story of Elijah in the mountain cave (1 Kings 19:11-13). Elijah was discouraged and thought he was left alone. He was wallowing in self-pity. He may have been extremely scared because his very life was threatened and, all around him, people were losing their lives, including the other prophets. He thought all hope was gone, but God visited him in his time of great despair.

It is vital for us to know and recognize God's voice. He speaks and reveals Himself in various ways, but so does the devil. Elijah sat on a mountain called Mount Horeb, which is also known as Mount Sinai (meaning, "the mount of revelation"), for God was going to reveal Himself to Elijah there. As he stood there, a great wind that broke rocks into pieces passed by. Can you imagine the power that must have been present? Yet the Lord was *not* in the wind. Then there was an earthquake—another powerful condition—but still the Lord was *not* in the earthquake. Then came fire. Fire burns, fire destroys, fire must be feared, but God was *not* in the fire. Following the fire, Elijah finally heard a still small voice, and as he listened, he recognized it was the Lord. He then got instructions as to what he should do and was assured there were many other prophets like himself still alive.

Here is what I learned from this story. In order to know and distinguish God's "still small voice," you must give yourself to Him fully and get to know Him well. *"My sheep hear my voice, and I know them, and they follow me,"* says John 10:27. I also learned that you have to possess great patience. A lack of it would have caused Elijah to run after the wind shouting, "Hey God, where are you going? I'm over here." That would have been a tragedy, because the wind would have blown him away like a rag doll, but patience and the knowledge of God conquered.

We get to know the Spirit through the Word, through prayer, and through worship and service to God. Let's challenge ourselves and enjoy this legacy! The need may arise for the Holy Spirit to be firm or aggressive or stern. Other times He speaks with authority and power. He also speaks warning through individuals.

In Acts 23:2-3, the high priest Ananias threatened that Paul should be struck on the mouth. Paul, speaking through the influence of the Holy Spirit, returned a firm word to him: "God will strike you, you whitewashed wall!" (vs. 3 NIV).

There is much spiritual warfare going on in the spirit realm, and at times you've got to be aggressive. Peter demonstrated this in Acts 8:18-23:

And when Simon saw that through laying on of the apostles' hands the Holy Ghost was given, he offered them money, Saying, Give me also this power, that on whomsoever I lay hands, he may receive the Holy Ghost.

Peter didn't smile and brush him off or ignore him. He confronted Simon (or the devil in him) immediately. Peter said to him,

...Thy money perish with thee, because thou hast thought that the gift of God may be purchased with money. Thou hast neither part nor lot in this matter: for thy heart is not right in the sight of God. Repent therefore of this thy wickedness, and pray God, if perhaps the thought of thine heart may be forgiven thee. For I perceive that thou art in the gall of bitterness, and in the bond of iniquity.

Wouldn't you say Peter had guts to stand there and say all this to Simon's face? These words were not written to Simon; they were told to him right where he stood. Along with Peter's bravery was the power of the Holy Spirit.

When the Holy Spirit inhabits our lives, He brings boldness and fierceness. When the Spirit needs to speak out, He will find a vessel He can use and will say what He wants to through that vessel. Some circumstances cause the Spirit to manifest great boldness, which creates authority and power in our lives, speech, or actions. You begin to feel as if you are the prime minister in charge of a country, or a king in charge of his kingdom. You lay down the rules, you instruct, you don't ask. You know you've got the right stuff inside you, and the awesome power of the Spirit is backing you up. Glory to God!

Peter was such person. Acts 4:8-10 says,

Then Peter, filled with the Holy Ghost, said unto them, Ye rulers of the people, and elders of Israel, If we this day be examined of the good deed done to the impotent man, by what means he is made whole; Be it known unto you all, and to all the people of Israel, that by the name of Jesus Christ of Nazareth, whom ye crucified... even by him doth this man stand here before you whole.

The Spirit does not cause us to fear. He gives us power over fear. *"For God has not given us the spirit of fear, but of power, and of love and of sound mind"* (2 Tim. 1:7).

Many of us are called ugly names by people who do not believe in the Holy Spirit as we do. When we allow the Holy Spirit to move in our lives, we may be called mad, unintelligent, foolish, weird, you name it; but as I once heard someone say, "I'd rather be a fool for Christ than a wise man for the devil."

As the Spirit fell on the disciples at Pentecost and they began to speak in other tongues, some of the people looking on mocked them and said they were drunk. The Bible says Peter stood up and countered them, saying,

These men are not drunk, as you suppose. It's only nine in the morning! No, this is what was spoken by the prophet Joel: "'In the last days, God says, I will pour out my Spirit on all people...'" (Acts 2:15-17 NIV).

There are times when we become careless and slack in our attitudes. We disregard the laws of life and the value of biblical directions. We become presumptuous in sin, and instead of repenting or changing our ways, we continue on the path that leads to destruction. The Lord never destroys a city or people without a warning of some sort (Sodom and Gomorrah in Genesis 18,19; Pharoah in the book of Exodus). Indeed, that is true; no matter how we rebel, God will always prolong His patience and give us a warning.

The Bible speaks of the dangerous results when we do not heed warning:

If when he see the sword come upon the land, he blow the trumpet, and warn the people; Then

whosoever heareth the sound of the trumpet, and taketh not the warning; if the sword come, and take him away, his blood shall be upon his own head (Ezek. 33:3-4).

So, there is safety in being obedient to warning.

And they said, Cornelius the centurion, a just man, and one that feareth God, and of good report among all the nation of the Jews, was warned from God by a holy angel to send for thee into his house, and to hear words of thee (Acts 10:22).

Now we exhort you, brethren, warn them that are unruly (1 Thess. 5:14). I remember, as a young believer growing up in church on the Island of Jamaica, we would walk circumspectly—watch our walk, and control our talk. If we told a lie, even a "white lie" as some of us phrase it, we would be troubled all week long because Sunday at church some Holy Ghost believer might yell it out in their manifestation. They didn't necessarily know who the person was that committed the sin; the Spirit just brought it out. Therefore, we were very careful to live a sanctified life as believers. These days, telling a lie, going to a party the night before church, backbiting, malice, or cursing, do not bother some of us. We just wipe off our mouths and brush ourselves off, put on our Sunday best, and boldly come into God's sanctuary feeling very comfortable. There is no one to warn, no one to discern, no one to cause us to tremble in our seats.

Backbiting, malice, and being two-faced are things in which the Holy Spirit is not present. You may be guilty of some or all of these. To regain your intimacy with Him, there must be a change. I get flabbergasted when I go to church and see believers intentionally hurting each other, or being devious. It is so sickening. This concerns me very much. I often wonder if we all read the same Bible and abide by the same principles as recorded in the Word of God. I know these words are a bit harsh, but if I can be instrumental in helping to make a change in someone's life, then this book has accomplished what it should.

If I would have taken to heart all the things some church people have done to me, I would have given up on God and the Church a long time ago. Thank God for the Holy Spirit who gives me strength and courage. The Bible says that the heart of man is desperately wicked (Jer. 17:9). There is great distrust in Christendom today. You go to the house of God and it's very hard to find someone trustworthy. I do not understand how believers, who preach the Word of God, read it, study it, sing it, share it with the unsaved and the sinful, yet still do not live it. Why can't we *live* the Word?

It's bad enough others discriminate against us as a people; what's worst is us discriminating against each other, even in the church, in the very presence of God. We fight against each other even after we shout the biggest "hallelujahs." The outside world uses guns, knives, etc. to kill, but we in the church use our tongues, eyes, and body gestures as weapons to destroy one another.

Many of us carry out these actions not knowing how serious the consequences are. The physical bodies of people with whom we interact may seem lively and in good health, but the inner man may be dying a slow agonizing death. Often, I do not have to turn my head around to know what's happening behind me; my spirit senses it. That's the thrill of having the Holy Spirit in our lives every day; He's very sensitive and alert.

Have you ever seen a cancer patient, particularly one who is new to the disease and in the first stages of it? Outside, the body looks great, but the cancer slowly kills that person from the inside unless detected early and treated. Similarly, that's what we do to our brothers and sisters when we backbite, criticize, and pull down others using our tongues. We need radical change. *"Walk in the Spirit, and ye shall not fulfill the lust of the flesh"* (Gal. 5:16).

> *Now no chastening for the present seemeth to be joyous, but grievous: nevertheless afterward it yieldeth the peaceable fruit of righteousness unto them which are exercised thereby* (Heb. 12:11).

When people do mean things to me, it troubles me a great deal. But when I reflect on the sacrifice Jesus made for us on the cross of Calvary while His own Father looked on and did nothing to rescue Him because of love, I realize I must go through trials on this earth. When I'm tempted to retaliate, the Holy Spirit, in His wisdom, whispers encouraging words through a song or the through the infallible Word of God.

I was about thirteen years old when I got saved. I do not recall meeting a brother or sister and not being able to look them in the eye. It didn't matter if they were as black as a tar baby or white as snow, or if they had one leg or one arm; it didn't matter if they were ugly or pretty—I could just accept them and love them. You see, we are able to rise above the natural when we see each other through the eyes of the Spirit. That kind of living is lacking these days. But why? If anything, we should become better people because we are getting the best of both worlds—the spiritual *and* the natural. So why aren't we? I believe it is because we sometimes value the natural more than the spiritual. We are so consumed by the attractions of the world that many of us don't have a clue what walking in the Spirit is about.

Do you need the Spirit to rule in your life? Ask Him; He's just a prayer away. *Now* is the time for change, so make the decision!

Let us be careful that our lifestyles and attitudes do not hinder those who have a desire to be in the Kingdom of God. The Lord blesses those who remain faithful to His Word and encourages those who are distressed and in pain. May the Holy Spirit be with us always as we keep looking at individuals through the eyes of the Spirit. God need us to carry out His work and keep each other in line. We need to wake up and be filled with the Spirit, holding on to the precious promises that come with His power in our lives.

CHAPTER SIX

He Detects the Enemies of Christ

THE GREATEST DETECTIVE IS the Holy Spirit. Neither the undercover cop, IRS, the international spy, nor the armies of the world could come close to performing the work of which the Holy Spirit is capable.

THE ENEMIES OF CHRIST

We've got three enemies that work together to destroy us: the world, the flesh, and the devil. In this particular chapter, my main focus is the devil. He is the main enemy of Christ and His followers. He wanted to kill our Saviour ever since He was a baby, and he kept trying even when Jesus became a grown man. In Matthew 4, we see how Jesus was tempted by the devil, and each time the devil would tempt Jesus, He was detected and combated.

The Holy Spirit detects the enemies of Christ. Only He can fathom Satan's cunning ways. The devil pretends to be a noble person who truly wants to help. He displays care and concern, but his secret agenda says something totally different than what his mouth says. As seen in Matthew 4, the devil wanted to defeat Jesus, and he waited until Jesus' flesh was weak. Being weak, Jesus could have succumbed to the devil, for even though Jesus was the Son of God, He was human like we are. However, during Jesus' testing, the Spirit was alert in Him and made the difference.

Let's look at the first test:

And when the tempter came to him, he said, If thou be the Son of God, command that these stones be made bread. But he answered and said, It is written, Man shall not live by bread alone, but by every word that proceedeth out of the mouth of God (Matt. 4:3-4).

Do you realize how wisely these words were put together? Jesus could have said, "No, I won't make bread," but even in His weakened state He was being a witness for his Father.

The second test is found in verses 5 and 6. The devil said to Jesus,

If thou be the Son of God, cast thyself down: for it is written, He shall give his angels charge concerning thee: and in their hands they shall bear thee up, lest at any time thou dash thy foot against a stone (vs. 6).

Then Jesus answered, in verse 7, "*It is written again, Thou shall not tempt the Lord thy God.*"

This test is fascinating! It shows you how difficult it is for the flesh to detect the devil. Flesh crumbles under the devil's devices, and only the Spirit stands strong in battle against him. Did you notice that the devil used the truth of the written Word and not lies? He will come to us with the very Word of God and use it in its proper context. But how are we going to penetrate these truths spoken by the devil and recognize him? The Holy Spirit, along with the knowledge of God's Word, will help us.

Look at the wisdom and authority with which Jesus answered Satan. He responded with the written Word which was really *His* Word, for He is God. He said, "You shall not tempt the Lord your God."

In verses 8 through 10 we see the third test:

All these things will I give thee, if thou wilt fall down and worship me. Then saith Jesus unto him, Get thee hence, Satan: for it is written, Thou shalt worship the Lord thy God, and him only shalt thou serve (vs. 9-10).

Guess what? All the things the devil was offering Jesus already belonged to Him. Besides, only the flesh would have needed those things; the Spirit had no use for what the devil was offering. Jesus was not in the flesh, He was in the Spirit. As we have already discussed, the Bible tells us to walk in the Spirit so we don't fulfill the lusts of the flesh.

You see, the flesh has carnal needs and desires, but the Spirit has spiritual needs and heavenly desires. The flesh succumbs to the devil every time, but the Spirit wars against him every time. This is how far the devil will go in order to feel like a somebody. He basically said to Jesus, "Get down on your knees and worship me and you will have it all." What a predicament—can you imagine? Satan is telling the King of Kings and Lord of Lords to worship him! Who does he think he is?

I grew up with my grandparents along with some cousins. Whenever we got in trouble, my grandmother would rush after us, but we would run faster than her and would often get away. This would happen again and again. My grandmother did not quarrel, but she had a famous saying: "I will let out the rope as far as you want, but you wait until I'm ready to reel it in." Believe me, we all knew exactly what that meant. Here's my purpose for telling this story: if you refer back to the first two tests, you will see that Jesus did not let the devil know that He knew it was him all along. But look at the last test. Jesus called the devil by name; He was ready to reel in the rope. As soon as Jesus verbalized the fact He knew it was Satan, Satan left Him and angels came and ministered to Him. Jesus won the battle, not through the flesh, but through the power of the Holy Spirit.

The devil has been an enemy of Christ from the beginning, and his agenda was to destroy Him. But each time the devil was detected and he failed in his attempts. Today, the devil often uses people to carry out his dirty jobs. When Jesus was born (Matt. 2), King Herod realized He was a great person and felt his kingship was threatened, so he came up with a rather sophisticated and cunning plan:

And he sent them [three wise men] *to Bethlehem, and said, Go and search diligently for the young child; and when ye have found him, bring me word again, that I may come and worship him also* (vs. 8).

Herod was a King whom others worshipped, and he had no intention of worshipping anyone, especially a baby. His trickery was soon found out. In verse 12, we read,

And being warned of God in a dream that they should not return to Herod, they departed into their own country another way.

When King Herod found out that the wise men had no intention of bringing him word about the child, he was very furious, and he took drastic measures of destruction:

Then Herod, when he saw that he was mocked of the wise men, was exceedingly wroth, and sent forth, and slew all the children that were in Bethlehem, and in all the coasts thereof, from two years old and under, according to the time which he had diligently enquired of the wise men (vs. 16).

Evidently, this mission of the devil failed.

Throughout Jesus' life and ministry, He experienced many threats, and thus had to constantly move to different places. He even faced opposition in His own country among His own people. *"A prophet is not without honour, save in his own country, and in his own house"* (Matt. 13:57). People called Him horrible names, but

71

each time He was able to defend Himself wisely, never sinning. Judas betrayed Him in the most cunning way you could think of—a kiss (Luke 22:48)—and although Jesus knew before hand that Judas would betray him with a kiss, Jesus didn't turn him away or try to prevent him from coming close. He allowed Judas to kiss Him. Once again, His incredible wisdom prevailed.

CHAPTER SEVEN

He Detects the Church—the Saints of God

THE CHURCH—THE SAINTS OF GOD

>*…Upon this rock I will build my church; and the gates of hell shall not prevail against it* (Matt. 16:18).

The Church as we know it is not a building of bricks, stones, and mortar. It is those of us who sincerely accept Christ as our Savior and serve and worship the Trinity that qualify as the Church. We, the Church, are bought with a price—the precious blood of Jesus Christ! Therefore, *"we are more than conquerors"* (Rom. 8:37). We are powerful and victorious because we are blood-bought and blood-washed. The Church has had enemies since its establishment. The moment you secretly or publicly confess Jesus as Lord, you automatically have an enemy—the devil. He loves company, and when you tell him you don't need his company anymore, he becomes furious. When he gets that way, you can expect a battle because he does not like the word "no." He hates rejection and his nature is to put up a fight.

Considering this, how are you going to counter-attack your enemy? Don't say, "I'll walk away," because he won't give up until he gets you. So, unless you choose to be defeated, you must retaliate. How do you retaliate against the devil?

Let's look at biblical believers and the struggles they went through at the hand of Satan. Daniel prayed three times each day in obedience to God and this action cost him. He was thrown into a den of lions but was not harmed because God was his protector (Dan. 6). Shadrach, Meshach, and Abednego were thrown into the fiery furnace because they chose not to bow down to false gods. Here again, God delivered them because of their faithfulness to Him. They were not harmed, though the fire was unusually hot and those who threw them in were burned (Dan. 3). Once again, God showed His greatness and power. He has sent a message to Satan that he cannot win when it comes to God's people. He may score some points, but in the end he still loses the battle.

Saul, whose name was later changed to Paul, was a per-secutor of the Church in his day. One day, God decided it was enough and He struck Saul down on the Damascus road. In Acts 9:4, Jesus spoke these words to him: *"Saul, Saul, why persecutest thou me?"* You might say *Saul* was attacking the Church, not the devil, but be reminded that Saul had to have been under the influence of the devil.

Notice also that this man who hated God and His people destroyed many lives because they believed in the name of Jesus. But the moment Jesus called this wicked man, Saul recognized that it was the Lord. *And he said, "Who art thou, Lord"* (vs. 5). Christian believers of all ages have been persecuted and martyred for the sake of Jesus and His gospel message.

Sometimes the devil's aim is to cause us to tear each other down and cause friction and division. Most times, when we finally realize it's the enemy, it's too late and the damage is already done—he's tricked us again. Still, in all this, he is a defeated foe because of the precious blood of Jesus Christ spilled on Calvary's cross for us. So when the devil thinks he's knocked us down and left us for dead, Jesus, in His love and mercy, picks us up and cleans us off, forgives our sins, and sends us on our way rejoicing. Isn't this wonderful?

Recently, worldwide prayer went out for the persecuted Church. Many stories were told by people who experienced persecution firsthand. Many who profess the name of Jesus live underground; they cannot live in the civilized world and confess Jesus as we have liberty to do in the West. It's a sad situation.

The question may arise in many of our minds as to where God is in all this. Why doesn't He come to their aid? Why does He continue to allow this to happen? There is no doubt in my mind that God is still in control. This universe is the devil's settlement for the time being, and his job is to tear down God's Kingdom every chance he gets. The Bible says, "...*your adversary the devil, as a roaring lion, walketh about, seeking whom he may devour*" (1 Pet. 5:8). Satan knows his time is limited here, so he and his followers are hastily working to accomplish their terrible deeds to break our faith and confidence in Christ before their time is expired.

We can defeat him by praying for one another, building up each other's faith, living in unity in Christ, and being educated, through the Word of God, of Satan's deceitful devices, so we can be on guard. Let us never forget: though Satan is the ruler of this world, God is watching him, and God is still in ultimate control of us all. We have nothing to fear, because the devil cannot go out of the boundaries of God's sight. Let us endeavour to focus on this marvelous assurance.

PART 3

What Changes Does He Bring About in Our Lives?

CHAPTER EIGHT

He Fights in Warfare

*A*RMIES OF THE WORLD combat wars using various artillery in order to triumph over their enemies. The more sophisticated their weapons, the greater the chance of victory.

Goliath thought he would have won the battle with David because of his strength, his armour, and the powerful prestige he made for himself among the countries and people of his time. But we realize in 1 Samuel 17 that this was not enough compared to what David had. David had the true and living God on his side. In verses 45-47 we read,

Then said David to the Philistine [Goliath], *Thou comest to me with a sword, and with a spear, and with a shield: but I come to thee in the name of the LORD of hosts, the God of the armies of Israel, whom thou hast defied. This day will the LORD deliver thee into mine hand; and I will*

smite thee, and take thine head from thee; and I will give the carcases of the host of the Philistines this day unto the fowls of the air, and to the wild beasts of the earth; that all the earth may know that there is a God in Israel. And all this assembly shall know that the LORD saveth not with sword and spear: for the battle is the LORD's, and he will give you into our hands.

Let me discuss another warfare in which God used angels to fight. The battle took place in the heavens between God's angel Gabriel and the devil and his angels. This was in regards to a message being sent from God to Daniel in answer to his prayers which the devil tried to intercept. This battle went on for twenty-one days, but guess who won in the end? Look at Daniel 10:12-14. The victory takes place in verse 14: *"Now I am come to make thee understand what shall befall thy people in the latter days: for yet the vision is for many days."* (In other words, the vision will take place in the future.) Satan was able to put a temporary stop on the answer to Daniel's prayer, but he could not keep it there forever. God always has backup in his warfare, so when Satan stopped Gabriel, God had to send the chief angel Michael to the rescue. If we read these truths and know them, why do we worry and become afraid of the enemy? We will not fight a losing battle if we allow God to fight it for us. Victory belongs to us when we trust God to fight for us.

We will now look at the spiritual warfare that the Holy Spirit fights for us. The moment we say "yes" to

Jesus and serve Him exclusively, we automatically are on battleground. We have no choice. We can either run or stand. If we run, we are shallow and don't know our God; if we stand, we are strong and know who we have on our side—the triune God.

A few years ago, I went to a Bible study class at a church where I had been a member. The pastor taught on the topic of the Holy Ghost. After listening in on some questions and answers, I suggested that the Holy Spirit also fights in warfare. I was surprised and dumbfounded to hear the reaction of the believers that followed. The Bible teacher basically said to me, "You can fight your warfare as long as it's in your little corner or closet." Almost everyone was laughing. I sat there totally astonished, wishing I had the guts and the words to back up my theory. I was broken.

When I left Bible study that night, I climbed into my vehicle, and the moment I drove out of the parking lot, I began to cry and talk to God as if He was sitting in the seat next to me. My house was twenty to thirty minutes from church, and I cried and talked to God until I pulled up in my driveway. I said, "God, I need to reach people with what I feel deep down in my heart. Why do I feel it but can't explain it?" In my frustration, I repeated three times, "Why can't I explain it?" When I reached home, my eyes felt swollen and my head ached, but I hid this from my family in the best way I could.

This happened during the middle of the week. The following Sunday I went to church "all prayed up." The service was electrifying—the Holy Spirit was awesome in that place. The choir was then called to minister. I have

81

to mention this about the choir, because as soon as they were assembled in the front of the altar getting ready to sing, I noticed something quite unusual. It was as if the choir members were specially selected that morning, because all the choir members who had been at the Bible study class and who had laughed when I spoke about warfare, were not among the choir members assembled to sing. What I heard next caused my eyes to pop and my mouth to drop open. The words of the song they were singing were the exact words I bellowed out in my question to God on my way home from the Bible study.

I got the answer I was yearning for. The song basically said that the Holy Spirit is like rivers of joy flooding my soul and I can't explain these rivers of joy (repeated three times). In that moment, I mustered all the strength I could to quench the power of the Spirit in my heart for a little while. Bowing my head, I said, "Thank You, Lord. You are with me after all. Thank You for answering my question."

By this time, I felt like I was about to explode, and out gushed the praises, the hallelujahs, and the skipping. My frail body felt as if it could not contain the power I was experiencing. The church was a powerhouse that Sunday morning.

I would love to report that things were fine and dandy afterwards, but it was not so. What happened next left me in tears and brought me to my knees in prayer and fasting. In fact, this book came into being as a result. It's truly amazing the things God allows to happen to us in order to accomplish His will and purpose in our lives.

I questioned what was meant by the statement "You can fight your warfare as long as it's in your little corner or closet." Did it mean people who were in trouble or needed spiritual deliverance should keep it to themselves or deal with it on their own? The Church is also a battleground and many hurting, sick people need help to battle the enemy. The Church cannot afford to let its people go to sorcerers; we have the power to help. We can denounce the devil, sickness, and any type of brokenness in the name of Jesus and gain the victory.

Marie is a beautiful sister in the Lord. She is blessed with the gift of prophesy. She said, "You are the weird one. That's what you will be considered when you are in the will of God and led by His Spirit." She talked about Elisha's story when he said, *"open his eyes that he may see"* (2 Kings 6:17). As Elisha looked, he realized that those who were for him were more than they who were against him. Marie continued, "The devil doesn't like it when a child of God speaks in tongues; he becomes intimidated."

The devil does not always tell or show us negative or unattractive things. His intent is for us to see the attractive and positive because he wants us to be comfortable and at ease in our slothful state. When we realize what is lacking in our spiritual growth, we will be able to fix it. But if we refuse God's message, we will remain in the state we are in and become stagnant. The Holy Spirit responds to the spiritual needs of God's people if they will listen, believe, and obey.

This warfare is one that does not need mechanical artillery. Neither does our battle against each other:

For we wrestle not against flesh and blood, but against principalities, against powers, against the rulers of the darkness of this world, against spiritual wickedness in high places (Eph. 6:12).

This warfare depicts the greatest enemy we have—the devil and his helpers.

When I was just a young believer growing up in my church in Jamaica, there were some fearless warfare battles fought. These battles were always fought by Spirit-filled prayer warriors. No wishy-washy jellyfish Christian could fight them. Sometimes many of us had to stay outside of the battle zone for our own protection. I learned great wisdom from these fighting Christian brothers and sisters. I was brought up in one of the best training camps in God's battleground. Hallelujah!

There was a sister in our church who was usually sick. She would fall in and out of sickness continually. She was on the brink of losing her mind. The worst thing about this situation was she had no known physical condition that could have triggered this illness. So she called for the Spirit-filled prayer warriors of the church. They came together and sang hymns, read Scripture, gave exhortations, as well as some encouraging words. This lead to prayer time, during which the power of the Holy Spirit broke loose in that house in a gushing way. It was the most beautiful and sweet experience, yet many of us trembled in our shoes. The whole place was filled with such an awesome, electrifying presence, we became almost fearful. The warriors ministered through the Spirit in tongues, rebukes, and commands for the defeat of the enemy and his hold on that sister's life. When they were finished, the woman who had been prayed over had a different countenance about her, a brighter one with her mind intact. To this very day, she has been well and living a full and free life in Christ. She was delivered.

There were many other similar battles fought, and God brought deliverance by the Holy Spirit through these Holy Ghost-filled prayer warriors.

We also fight warfare as individuals. Not long ago, I became very discouraged. My emotions were running wild, I had decisions which I had a hard time dealing with. I became fearful and felt the best thing to do was to run. But one particular Sunday, I visited a church and was impressed the moment I stepped out of my car. It was raining, and I saw a brother standing at the door of the church (this was the back entrance). As I started walking toward the church, he started walking toward me with a huge umbrella. I looked to see who was behind me, but there was no one. He must have seen my gesture, because he promptly said, "I've come for you." Well, I felt special immediately! He was there doing his duty for God by sheltering all those who didn't have an umbrella. Jesus said in Matthew 8:10, *"I have not found so great faith, no, not in Israel."* When I saw such unselfish hospitality being performed in church, I felt obliged to say, "I have not seen such polished etiquette, no, not in Zion."

That was just the beginning. The worship service was refreshing, and the preaching! Well, it was as if an angel followed me there and whispered everything I was going through in the pastor's ears. First, I was told the things I was experiencing (I can personalize this because I believe that message was for me). He spoke about fear, self-esteem, discouragement, and more. Then he explained how to deal with those circumstances.

This is where spiritual warfare comes in. Pastor Fisher related something I had never quite grasped before; he said, "These conditions are spirit-related and should be dealt with spiritually. You have to call each condition by its name and say, 'Spirit of fear, I come against you in the name of Jesus! Spirit of discouragement, I come against you in the name of Jesus!' Name them one by one and don't leave any out."

Then he preached about running away from our problems. I started feeling uncomfortable in my seat; this was too real. He said, "You who are planning to run away from facing your battles, stop!" He told the story of David and Goliath and stated that if David had turned and run, he would have been a dead man. He reminded me to put on the whole armour of God and pointed out that the armour covers only the front of a soldier; however, there is no protection for the back. This means you must face the enemy and you will have a chance; but the moment you run, your unprotected back is a prime target for the enemy.

In our time of individual warfare, let us first recognize that the enemy brings on these conditions to break us.

Then denounce them in the name of Jesus. I thanked God for Pastor Fisher because now I know how to handle the enemy's darts. Whenever I'm in church or anywhere else and someone chooses to be unkind or mean, I just silently call the action by its name and say, "Spirit of... (use the name of the trial you are facing), I denounce you in the name of Jesus," and I feel a gush of peace about me instead of hurt and pain. Try it; it works.

It is absolutely essential that you feed the spirit man with the Word of God, because you need the Word in battle; that's your sword. The enemy doesn't like to hear the Word, and if you don't know it, you cannot use it as a weapon to fight the enemy. The Bible says,

> *For the word of God is quick, and powerful, and sharper then any twoedged sword, piercing even to the dividing asunder of soul and spirit, and of the joints and marrow, and is a discerner of the thoughts and intents of the heart* (Heb. 4:12).

Some of our biggest battles take place at night while we sleep. The adversary is never asleep, and neither is our spirit. The Holy Spirit fights battles for us while we sleep.

I have fought many spiritual battles in my sleep. I have even woken up speaking in tongues. Usually I mumble when I wake from sleep, but in tongues I speak very clearly because my spirit speaks. My body sleeps, but my spirit is alert and aware of what is going on around me.

God also has His protective agents taking care of us, whether we sleep or not. The Bible says in Psalm 34:7, *"The angel of the LORD encampeth round about them*

87

that fear him, and delivereth them." The children of God can rest comfortably, even in slumber, because we have a watchful eye always in our corner: *"When the enemy shall come in like a flood, the Spirit of the LORD shall lift up a standard against him"* (Isa. 59:19). Why do we not need to be afraid of the adversary?...

> *Thou shalt not be afraid for the terror by night; nor for the arrow that flieth by day; Nor for the pestilence that walketh in darkness; nor for the destruction that destroys at noonday* (Ps. 91:5-6).

We are totally covered and nothing can break that cover unless God allows it. Look up the following Scripture which assure us of our protection: Psalm 23:4; Psalm 27:2; Psalm 91:10-11. Aren't you thrilled you have full coverage?

CHAPTER NINE

He Draws the Hearts of Men to God

It is the spirit that quickeneth; the flesh profiteth nothing: the words that I speak unto you, they are spirit, and they are life (John 6:63).

SPIRIT-FILLED TEST FOR A TRUE BELIEVER

1. Examine a believer's life by the manifestation of the fruit of the Spirit.

- ※ Is there true love for God, the things of God, and the people of God?

- ※ Is there quality time for communion, worship, and fellowship with Christ?

- ※ Is there enthusiasm when studying the Scriptures?

- ※ When a believer chooses to dislike another because of his/her sincerity to follow and obey Christ, he or she lacks the Holy Spirit.

✳ If you remain in sin and continue to walk according to the flesh, the Holy Spirit is not in you. Instead, the devil is the active one in your life.

✳ If you turn from sin and faithfully obey Christ, you assuredly possess the Holy Spirit, and He will remain in your life if you continue to sanctify Him in your heart.

✳ You have the Spirit of God when you have a burning desire to be a witness for Christ by leading others to Him.

✳ When you genuinely have the Holy Spirit, you will be receptive to the Spirit's operation within the Kingdom of God and His gifts in your life, especially the gift of speaking in tongues, which is the initial outward sign of the baptism in the Spirit (Acts 2:4,6-18,43).

Any assumed baptism in the Spirit that does not result in the manifestations of the Spirit in our lives is an obvious departure from the experience of New Testament believers and the example presented in the book of Acts.

I detect that in many churches, when it comes to financial and numerical success, ministers of the gospel steer their congregation to adapt principles laid down by others, instead of following biblical principles and allowing God to use individuals as they are. Don't get me wrong; there are examples we can learn from others that will bring us great success, but let it not be at the expense of watering down the Word or putting the Holy Spirit on the back burner. I'm black and a native of West India, so I can speak for my kind. Can you fathom going into a church with our kind of people and finding no action—

people motionless, silent, and the Holy Spirit nowhere to be found?

I love to be in the company of learned and educated people. They, as well as the less fortunate, are needed in the Church; we all need each other. I don't mind associating with brethren who may not have had the opportunity to educate themselves and become wise and fluent in their speech. It doesn't matter, for many of these people are genuine in their walk with God.

We do not have to quench the Spirit in order to attract a large crowd or certain kinds of people. We just need to show genuine love and appreciation for each other. We need to be sympathetic, compassionate, and understanding. In addition, the preacher needs to be filled with the anointing of the Holy Spirit, so when the Word is preached, it connects with the hearts of God's people.

God knew what He was doing when He made people of different colours and races. I believe colours meant something to God. Perhaps God looked at blacks and said, "You will be people of rhythm and zest. You will need excitement to accompany your blackness."

God made all races unique, so black men don't need to try to act like white men in order to be successful. We are emotional people, and we love excitement. If we try the more subtle way, we will be bored and feel empty and unfulfilled because we will be stifling our nature. Wouldn't life be boring if God made us all the same in every aspect of our being? Let's enjoy our variety as God intended; we will be surprised yet pleased at the results.

I have noticed a favourable quality among big churches that have a majority of white leadership. These churches have a technique which others are now adopting. I observed the way they welcome people into their congregation. It doesn't matter who you are or what you look like, you are greeted with a big smile, a firm handshake, and an encouraging word of welcome before you enter the sanctuary. Many people are drawn to these churches, even people from my race, because they were offered what we did not offer.

Salvation is the best remedy for a sin-sick soul. It is a gift above all others. It is possible only through Jesus. He said, *"I am the way, the truth and the life: no man cometh unto the Father, but by me"* (John 14:6). Salvation is received by grace, through faith in Jesus Christ:

> *For by grace are ye saved through faith; and that not of yourselves: it is the gift of God: Not of works lest any man should boast* (Eph. 2:8-9).

When we are drawn to God through this incredible transformation, it changes everything in our lives. It changes our walk, talk, attitude, direction, goals, and priorities because we become directed by the Word of God and answer to the Lord of our lives, Jesus Christ.

In order for our hearts to be quickened by the Spirit and drawn to God, we must go through a process. We must come to the realization that we need to be born again. The term "born again" is best described in John 3, which tells the story of a Pharisee named Nicodemus. During his conversation with Jesus, Jesus says to Nicodemus,

Verily, verily, I say unto thee, Except a man be born of water and of the Spirit, he cannot enter into the kingdom of God (vs 5).

What steps do we take in this born-again process? This is where witnessing comes in. Believers should tell others about Christ and His saving grace. Some souls might not have any other access to Christ's word except for what they hear from us. We are God's messengers; we have the truth. Our goal should be to educate ourselves in the Word of God and to seek the appropriate approach to deal with individuals according to their unique ways and attitudes in order to lead them to Christ.

Everyone is different, so we must witness accordingly. The Bible says, *"He that winneth souls is wise"* (Prov. 11:30). When the word or seed (Matt. 13:3-8) is sown, it is not your duty to save that person; you can't! That job is for the Holy Spirit who works on the heart. He draws people to the Father. So, you see, our job is really not as hard as we fear it to be. *"And you hath he quickened, who were dead in trespasses and sins"* (Eph. 2:1). It takes a quickening by the Spirit to be brought back to life from this kind of death.

No matter how cold and dried out we get by sin or because we lack the Word of God, we can be revived by the Spirit. He is the Special Doctor you need when it comes to spiritual health. It was Ezekiel who was asked this very important question: *"...can these bones live?"* (Ezek. 37:3). God's answer is found in verse 14: *"And shall put my spirit in you, and ye shall live...."* Ezekiel wondered if those useless bones could come to life again and God assured him they could by His Spirit.

It doesn't matter how low a person gets, or how vile and wicked, there is always hope for him. We tend to pass our own judgment on people by the way they look, dress, or act, but it's not up to us to choose who God can use or who is worth saving. All we need to do is be obedient to the call of God and do our duty by sharing the Word to every creature, and the Holy Spirit will give life and do the drawing. Let's stop looking at how dry the bones are and start focusing on the fact that God is well able to put breath, sinews, and flesh on these bones by His Spirit.

I challenge every believer to be true to the call of God. In obedience, GO! Go tell it, preach it, exhort it, sing it, dance it, live it, walk it, talk it, share it in whatever way or form you can minister the Word of God to the lost. Then stand back and watch the Holy Spirit move by His power to quicken the hearts of men and draw them to God. It will be a great time of harvest. *Praise the Lord!*

About the Author

MY NAME IS NYSLEY DINNALL. I became a born-again Christian at the age of thirteen. Praise God, He's been with me ever since! I was born in Jamaica in the parish of St. Catherine in a little district called West Prospect. I suffered many things due to deprivation. Fortunately, God was always with me.

Our family was better off than most villagers in our district, but we were still poor. I hardly had enough money to buy lunch at school or for books to study in order to take exams, but I was determined to get an education regardless of my unfortunate circumstances. Often, I studied by borrowing other children's books, or I would remain after school to do my homework because I couldn't afford my own books.

Through all this, I tasted a little of my dreams. I enrolled in a teacher's course through the Jamaican Youth Corp. and taught as a teacher's assistant for a year, after which I had the opportunity to come to Canada (a land of prosperity). Everything was in my reach, nevertheless, I faced a few obstacles.

Many circumstances shattered my dreams, but not totally. I'm always learning. Recently, I achieved a secretarial certificate and a diploma as a teacher's aide through ICS. I've been to a few colleges and have taken other subjects such as English, bookkeeping, accounting, and basic computer skills to upgrade my education. My most recent endeavour was obtaining a Microsoft certificate. I went to night school for approximately three years for this course, and finally I succeeded. God has been good to me.

I've always enjoyed writing. The moment I take time out to write, my mind is flooded with ideas and racing much faster than my pen. When I attended school in Jamaica, I was one of the students selected from my class to read my essay for the entire school. A few years ago, I took a refresher course in English at Centennial College and my end-of-term grade was an "A." I realized I had not lost my love for writing which encouraged me a great deal. I am particularly pleased to be making full use of it by writing this book.

God gave me a fabulous family—my husband Lester and my adorable and beautiful children, Brian, Alicia, and Caroline. We own a wonderful home, a growing business, and enjoy a fantastic life together. We are doing very well because God is a part of our lives. Amidst all this, the most precious thing to me is the fact that I accepted the Lord Jesus as my Saviour, and the highlight of my life is the service I do for Him in whatever direction it leads me.